LONG EATON
THEN & NOW

KEITH REEDMAN

SUTTON PUBLISHING

Sutton Publishing Limited
Phoenix Mill · Thrupp · Stroud
Gloucestershire · GL5 2BU

First published 2004

Copyright © Keith Reedman, 2004

Title page photograph: Long Eaton town
centre, 2003.

British Library Cataloguing in Publication Data
A catalogue record for this book is available from the
British Library.

ISBN 0-7509-2993-6

Typeset in 10.5/13.5 Photina.
Typesetting and origination by
Sutton Publishing Limited.
Printed and bound in England by
J.H. Haynes & Co. Ltd, Sparkford.

Lace factories along the Erewash canal, 2003.

Opposite: The famous Rowell's shop, High Street, 1981.

CONTENTS

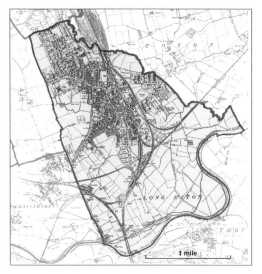

Long Eaton's historic boundaries.

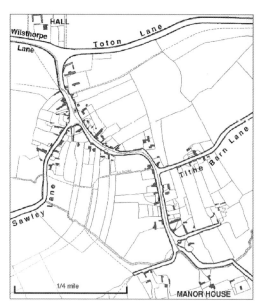

Long Eaton village, *c.* 1830.

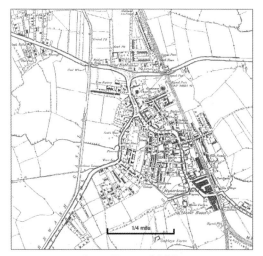

Long Eaton, 1880.

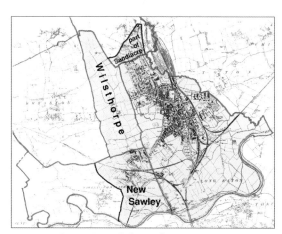

Long Eaton's boundaries, 1921.

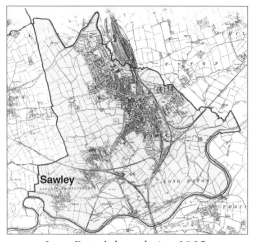

Long Eaton's boundaries, 1935.

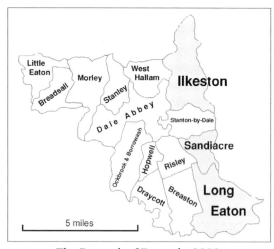

The Borough of Erewash, 2003.

INTRODUCTION

Long Eaton is not an 'historic' town. Many well-known Derbyshire towns such as Buxton or Ashbourne are only a fraction of Long Eaton's size but are nationally known. The reason for Long Eaton's relative obscurity is that the industry and product which brought about the town's phenomenal growth and prosperity during the late nineteenth century was machine-made lace, universally known as Nottingham lace, even though most of it was made in Long Eaton.

The town's recorded history starts, as with most settlements in England, in the Domesday Book of 1086. Before this we must use archaeological and circumstantial evidence, such as the name of the settlement. Sufficient archaeological finds have been discovered to establish that people were active here five thousand years ago but a settlement called Eaton was probably not made until the sixth century AD by Anglian people who originated in the Schleswig-Holstein district of northern Germany. The name 'Eaton' is usually translated as 'farm between streams' or 'watery farm' – and watery it is. Most of its land was, until recent flood defences, readily inundated by the surrounding rivers: Trent on the south, Derwent on the west and Erewash on the east. During the eighth century the Midlands were invaded by the Danes and it is highly probable that a contingent of them settled locally: Wilsthorpe, on Long Eaton's edge, is a Danish name. Crucially, the 'Eaton' of Domesday records a large proportion of freemen who were likely to have been descendants of the Danish settlers. Freemen were able to own and sell their land and this was subsequently very important when, during the nineteenth century, land was needed for industrial expansion. There was no 'squirearchy' to prevent development and land was freely available.

Before this later development, 'Eaton' grew only very slowly as a small, self-governing, agricultural village. By 1288 it had become Long Eaton, probably because it had extended in a southward straggle from the church along the course of a small stream, now culverted below High Street and Main Street. When the first census of the country was taken in 1801 Long Eaton had a population of 504 – similar to the surrounding villages of Breaston, Draycott, and Sandiacre. Sawley's population was a third greater, but it was a village with few owner occupiers and was economically poorer.

The Erewash Canal, cut from the River Trent to the Derbyshire coalfield in 1777, was part of the Industrial Revolution but although the canal passed through the length of Long Eaton there is no evidence of any resulting development, except at Trent Lock where the canal joins the river. The coming of the railways, in the 1830s and '40s, was a different matter. Shortly after the Erewash Valley Railway was constructed through the village in 1847 as an improved means of exporting Derbyshire coal, things started to happen. On the northern edge of the village the Midland Railway built a weighing facility for coal wagons which eventually grew into Toton marshalling yard, one of the country's largest. In the village itself the Manor House estate, which had been split by the railway, was sold to Samuel Claye who built a railway wagon manufacturing works. Both these railway developments brought demand for labour and housing which the village had to accommodate by expansion, and both Claye and the Midland Railway built houses for their employees.

The Market, 1971.

Before the railway development there had been another nascent industry. The East Midlands was the home of the stocking knitting industry – a cottage industry until well on in the nineteenth century. The earliest record of a framework knitter in Long Eaton is 1677 but the town was not a major centre. During the early years of the nineteenth century the manufacture of machine-made lace was developed in Nottingham using modified knitting frames. Use of these machines spread across the region and even by 1830 there were nine lace manufacturers in Long Eaton. These were mainly farmers, operating a sideline with the then hand-operated machines. It was not long before steam power was applied to the machines and they became progressively larger. The first steam-driven machines were installed here in 1834, but expansion was slow.

In Nottingham the development of the lace machine continued, especially after the mid-nineteenth century, but space for them ran out. The small workshops where the machines were operated would not hold the newer large machines and Nottingham was bursting at the seams, and at that time prevented from expanding. So the surrounding towns and villages where development could take place were able to take advantage. In Long Eaton two multi-storey steam-powered factories were erected during the 1850s, and by 1860 the town's population had risen to over 1,500; still only a large village, but well outstripping its neighbours. During the 1860s and 1870s there was a steady stream of lace manufacturers moving production from Nottingham to Long Eaton. Local firms also expanded so that by 1881 the population had risen to over six thousand. By this time few of the old village's buildings remained and the suburbs were rising rapidly. There was no water supply and no proper drainage – but there was a health problem. Provision of proper services was secondary to keeping the rates as low as possible, and the manufacturers were in the seats of power on the Local Board of Health.

During the 1880s industrial expansion was frenetic, with many huge multi-storey, steam-powered lace factories being built, especially alongside the canal, and with them housing estates to cope with the influx of workers. The railway was expanding too and by 1901 the population had doubled in twenty years to over 13,000. Fortunately, the Local Board had been forced to provide a water supply and this was available in 1892, although main drainage was not generally available for many years after that.

In 1894 English local government was reorganised and Long Eaton became an urban district (LEUDC), governed by an elected council. In 1921 and 1934 Long Eaton's boundaries were extended to include Wilsthorpe, Sawley and part of Sandiacre. The Urban District Council continued to govern until the national reorganisation of 1974, when Long Eaton was merged into the District of Erewash which later became the Borough of Erewash.

The opening of the Long Eaton electricity station in 1902 spelt the end of building multi-storey lace factories. Single-storey, shed-type factories could use electric power economically and many of these were built in the decade before the First World War. At that time there were about 1,400 lace machines operating in the town and over 4,000 people were directly employed from a population which in 1911 had reached almost 20,000. The war put a temporary halt to the expansion of the industry, but afterwards it was boom again. Unfortunately, the balloon was about to burst. In 1920 the industry collapsed: fashion, cotton prices and tariffs were all to blame and by 1923 the industry was halved. It continued in slow decline until the last traditional lace manufacturer closed in 2001, but there are still a few lace firms in the town.

As the factories were emptied of lace machines, new industries sprang up to fill the spaces. The most successful of these has been the upholstered furniture industry for which the town is now pre-eminent. In 1920 Elson & Robbins started manufacturing seating springs in Long Eaton and in the same year the Slater Resilient Upholstery company was founded. The following year F.C. Wade started his well-known upholstery business. These three firms between them have spawned most of the many furniture manufacturers, past and present, in Long Eaton. Today there are dozens.

Several other major firms started up in the town near the time of the lace industry's collapse. The well-known 'Leisure' steel sink manufacturer, founded by W.A. Wallis, son of a lace machine manufacturer, started in 1921. Concordia, an electric wire manufacturer, moved from London into a Sawley lace factory in 1916. A piano industry which started in 1920 only ceased in 1998, and later re-started a few miles away in Trowell.

Because Long Eaton grew so rapidly, few of its residents can claim to be of long-standing families. The large immigrant population of the late nineteenth and early twentieth centuries was not slow to organise itself. Much of the population was Nonconformist, still evidenced by the large number of Methodist and other Nonconformist chapels. It was a liberal, egalitarian society with a very strong Co-operative movement. There were, of course, the bosses, but they had invariably risen from similar roots and many were of a similar persuasion. Long Eaton was accurately described in the early twentieth century as a 'cultural democracy'.

Recreational facilities have been well provided in the town. West Park, the earliest part of which was purchased for the townspeople in 1905, is a large, centrally placed public park containing facilities for most sports and an indoor swimming pool. In 1906 the town's Carnegie Library opened.

Today the town still thrives with a multitude of industries as well as being a dormitory town for the neighbouring cities of Nottingham and Derby. With the M1 motorway on its doorstep, it is still a communications hub. Warehousing facilities are among the newer industries along with high technology engineering, information technology and electronics.

Having been such a small, nondescript village at the time when photography was in its infancy, Long Eaton was poorly recorded by the medium until the end of the nineteenth century. The oldest datable photograph in this book is of the parish church of St Laurence, taken just before it was rebuilt in 1868. Otherwise, the majority of the early pictures were taken during the first decade of the twentieth century, by which time most of the old village properties had been demolished, leaving a handful to be recorded. The Manor House, which survived until about 1900, was not among them but it is evident that much of the old village had consisted of a mixture of brick and timber-framed, thatched roof, farmhouses and cottages. The Market Place and High Street still have most of their Victorian and Edwardian buildings, though sadly most of the original shop fronts have gone. Recently pedestrianised and designated as a Conservation Area, there is hope that the town centre will become less vulgar as the worst excesses of retailers are curbed.

Apart from the virtually complete takeover of our streets by the motor vehicle and its attendant street clutter, the main feature which is noticeable in the 'now' photographs is the extent to which trees obscure much of what was previously visible – a mixed blessing in some cases, but we have a town to be proud of in many respects.

Keith Reedman
Long Eaton, 2004

Posed with pig iron in front of the melting cupola, foundry men at Claye's Wagon Works in the early 1900s.

1

Hall Green & Market Place

For many centuries the farm on the Beeches site on the south-east side of The Green
was the northern limit of habitation. It was not until after Long Eaton's land was
enclosed in 1769 that development began outside the old confines. One of the first
to build was Henry Howitt, who constructed a new grand farm and farmhouse near
The Green in 1778. The Green is the area at the junction of Nottingham and Derby
Roads with the Market Place. Now a traffic island, it is remembered for having had a
stone-built public convenience in the centre which was popularly known as 'Haddon
Hall'. Its predecessor, a cast-iron dome-topped gents urinal, was nicknamed 'St
Paul's'. The Market Place which contains the parish church is the ancient centre of
Long Eaton. The church, which until 1829 was a chapel to Sawley, is on one of the
highest spots of the old settlement area. Although not susceptible to flooding, it was
damaged in a fire which in 1696 destroyed fourteen houses in the vicinity. This
aerial view, looking south-east, was taken in about 1963.

The Hall and its associated buildings comprised the home and farm of gentleman farmer Henry Howitt. It was built in 1778 in what had been a common pasture before the land was enclosed in 1767 and awarded to John Howitt, Henry's brother. The building has been attributed to the Derby architect Joseph Pickford. The Howitts sold the property in 1839 to the Revd Francis Gawthorne, whose heirs sold it to Joseph Fletcher, a lace manufacturer. In 1921 the Hall was bought by Long Eaton Urban District Council for a town hall, a function it now performs for Erewash Borough Council along with the 1991 extension. The earlier photograph shows a bay window under construction and possibly a Miss Fletcher.

The older picture of about 1920 is captioned 'Cattle Market'. Was this the locals having a joke with the photographer? The quantity of railings which surround the public conveniences on The Green had led to the 'cattle market' nickname. The view is from the Market Place towards the junction of Nottingham and Derby Roads. The Hall can be seen in the left background and Barclays bank, by the Long Eaton architect Ernest Ridgeway, is on the left. The bank building, constructed in 1898 for the Derby & Derbyshire bank, is relatively unspoiled.

William Brentnall and his brother George are among those pictured with their Christmas display of 1904. The Brentnalls had a butchery business in the town from the 1870s until the 1950s, and had their own slaughterhouse at the rear of these premises. Part of the original shop is still occupied by one of the few remaining independent butchers in the town. Many modern shop fronts have the saving grace of original features on the first floor: not these.

The town centre in 1928. The gas works and gas holders, top right, have now gone along with Austin's lace factory complex (latterly Jones Stroud) to the right of centre. All the housing formed by the cross of Union Street and Waverley Street to Cross Street has been demolished. Trent Works, which was for many years Wallis & Longden's lace machine manufactory, in the right centre, has been replaced with the now demolished Waverley Mills. The market has been moved to the garden area in the bottom centre. At the top, left of centre, Asda now occupies what was the Midland Railway housing estate and goods yard.

The north end of Market Place, 1904. On the left is part of Marshall's Trent Brewery, converted into shops in 1928. Next, with the tall stacks (now sadly truncated), is the Midland Counties District bank of 1903, now part of the Grade II Listed York Chambers, an outstanding example of Arts & Crafts architecture by Long Eaton architects, Gorman & Ross. The building on the right centre with three gables is the Nottingham & Nottinghamshire bank (now NatWest) of 1903 by John Sheldon of Long Eaton. The studio which published the postcard has partly erased a group of pedestrians on the left.

These wooden shops on the corner of Regent Street were photographed during the 1890s. Butcher James Daniels, who lived in the farmhouse where the present NatWest bank is sited, stands with George Smith, a lace manufacturer whose machines were in Orchard's factory. On the pony is butcher's boy Jack Roberts who later had his own shop. In the background is the Conservative Club and Joseph Borebanks' lace machine workshops. The workshop and the shops were demolished in 1900 to make way for the existing buildings. The Yorkshire bank occupation is recent – the shop was a furniture showroom for much of the twentieth century. The Conservative Club is now Jim Brennan's public house.

This picture of St Laurence's church is the oldest known photograph of Long Eaton. The view is of the church as it was before being completely rebuilt (with the exception of the tower and spire) in 1868 to the designs of the prominent Victorian architect G.E. Street. The gate pillars and wall (without railings since 1942) date from about 1860 when the almshouses which occupied the area in front of the churchyard were demolished. The wall was altered in 1921 when the War Memorial designed by J.N. Comper was erected.

A view of the Market Place taken from the first-floor window of the former Refuge building next to the church. The date is not certain but it would have been about 1900. The dilapidated cottages next to the Old Cross Inn in the centre were demolished in 1908. The gap was partly filled by Electra House in 1922 but the site next to it was not built on until 1975 for the Loughborough Building Society. On the right is the HSBC (formerly Midland) bank, built in 1889 for the Nottingham Joint Stock bank (architect A.N. Bromley of Nottingham) which previously had premises on the corner of Bank Street. It is now listed Grade II.

The Palace was built on a vacant Market Place plot in 1913 (architect J. Dodd of Long Eaton) to replace the 'Tin Trunk' Palace Theatre in Queen Street. It was re-fronted in 1936 to the form shown opposite and in 1965 was renamed the Ritz. In 1986 the name was changed again to the Screen; it closed as a cinema in 1996 and has just reopened as a pub, named after the fictitious Litten Tree.

Although Lionel Austin, the last member of the Austin family to run the shop (left) which adjoins the HSBC bank, died in 1987, the shop has remained unchanged but is now closed. The picture was probably taken in about 1900. The later shop front (opposite) dates from before the First World War and is likely to remain unaltered when new owners move in.

The north-west side of the Market Place has changed little since the Palace was built between the bank and the Old Bell public house. The Old Bell is probably the oldest public house in the town and the basis of the present two-storey part probably dates from just before 1700. Once an external staircase on the front led to a room which was used both as a public meeting room and as a schoolroom. The NatWest bank on the right was built in 1903 after the farmhouse which had stood there since 1693 was demolished. The architect for the bank was J. Sheldon of Long Eaton, whose family had been builders in the town for many years.

This building was the last recognisably old house in the town to survive. Built in 1693, the year when many of Long Eaton's houses in the Market Place were built to replace those destroyed in a fire, it was demolished in 1963. Many townspeople were dismayed by the demolition, but this was at a time when few buildings had any statutory protection and the local council simply did not care enough about conservation. The building had its thatch replaced with slate by Mr Savage who was the last occupier of what he called 'The Bacon Shop'.

In the centre is Mount Tabor Methodist chapel, which was built in 1884 as a replacement for an earlier chapel on the same site. This was the only Nonconformist chapel in the town to have its own burial ground. When the building was demolished in about 1961 the remains and memorials were removed to the Lime Grove cemetery. The replacement building was a block of shops and offices in the Festival of Britain style, which has worn rather well. More impressive is Therm House, built on the site of the small shops in 1938 for the Long Eaton Gas Company. This fine Modernist-style building by the Long Eaton architects Dodd & Wilcox was the gas showroom until very recently. Upstairs is a large hall which was for many years the Oxford Restaurant.

Market Place *c.* 1935, just before the gas company built Therm House (see p. 21). The spire of St Laurence's church can just be seen behind what is now the Halifax Bank. The bank was built in 1889 for Messrs Samuel Smith & Co.'s Nottingham bank to the designs of the Mansfield-born architect Fothergill Watson, many of whose idiosyncratic buildings adorn Nottingham. This one is a fine Grade II listed building from early in his career before he reversed his names. No longer a car park on non-market days, the pedestrianised area is now mainly the haunt of pigeon feeders.

The south-west corner of Market Place leading into Tamworth Road, *c.* 1960. On the left is Oddfellows Hall, which had three shops on the ground floor; it was built in about 1882 on the site of one of the town's first Methodist churches. From the left, just in view, is Nellie Marshall's dress shop, then Price's fishing tackle shop followed by Offiler Brothers, grocers (formerly Wolley). First in the next block is Russell's cycle shop, then T.W. Salt, sweets and tobacco (formerly Mrs Swann), next Jeffs & Walker, radio and TV (formerly Nequests music), and lastly Brockett & Sons, butchers (formerly Cyril Redgate and before that James Daniels (see page 15)). The last little shop was part of the butcher's. The new shops, which are not a visual attraction, were set back for road widening which never happened.

The market in 1971 flourished with temporary stalls, put up every week for the Friday and Saturday markets. At this time the road through the town was the A453 Nottingham to Birmingham road, still following the route of the old turnpike road. Fortunately traffic was not so dense then. The market, which was made official in 1881, was transferred to a site off Beaconsfield Street in 1973 and the area, along with High Street, was pedestrianised in 1995. The three-storey building on the right was built in 1922 for the electrical engineer F.W. Ames and was acquired in 1931 by the LEUDC's electricity department. After nationalisation in 1948 it became the local showroom and office of the East Midlands Electricity Board. It is now a chemist's shop.

2

High Street to Manor Green

The main historic town street follows the course of an ancient stream, along which Long Eaton developed. The stream is now culverted, but its course is now the main commercial thoroughfare of the town. Most of the town's historic development and redevelopment has taken place from Hall Green in the north by way of the Market Place, High Street and Main Street to Manor Green in the south.

The west side of High Street, *c.* 1906. There were thirteen shops between the man hanging mats at Simmons (clothier and pawnbroker) and the Market Place. The three-storey block was built in about 1880 and has four shops, the last of which is H. Eales, jeweller, still trading. Others early in the century included S.T. Parker (cycle maker), E.C. Lewin (picture framer), W. Smith (herbalist), and A. Mellors (fruiterer). The present Bon Marché is the remnant of the five-shop block whose former occupiers included Parker and J. & H. Lacey. The Abbey National building society is one of the few quality new buildings in the area. The large flat-roofed building, now occupied by Dorothy Perkins, was built during the 1960s for the electrical goods firm of C. Gilbert, which had first occupied Lewin's shop. Between Perkins and Eales are now a bookmaker and a charity shop.

The east side of High Street during the 1980s before the redevelopment of Austin's lace factories (the Jones Stroud site). This is the only part of the scheme with any character; unfortunately it did not include the next pair of unsightly shops. The last building before the three-storey block in the Market Place dates from the first half of the nineteenth century. It was a dwelling house of the Austin family which owned the lace factories at the rear, and it was here that their public house was located. Name changes are nothing new; it was the Joiners Arms in 1837 and the Durham Ox by 1848, both now long forgotten.

The house with the added shop front was originally the home of Thomas Smith, lace manufacturer, whose factory was immediately behind it. The shop front had been added before the First World War and for many years was Marsden, grocers. The next building was well decorated with red terracotta detailing and balustrading between the gables, which carried the date 1914. Mister Minit had a shop in this building, as did Laceys who also occupied the factory at the rear. The whole site was redeveloped in 1989 with a well-designed replacement.

The east side of the High Street, *c.* 1920. On the left is Hose Bros (outfitters), followed by Butterfield's Drapery Stores and the next shop, now Ladbrokes, was also Butterfield's. The next block which contained Granger's drapery and Coombs boot repairers was replaced during the 1960s with a shop that was originally Burton's grocery, then Fine Fare, now Superdrug. The tall chimney in the background belongs to Smith's lace factory (see p. 45). On the extreme right is a cane chair suspended on a shop front with a price label which looks like 2s.

George Button, a tinsmith, opened this shop in 1862 and is seen here in about 1906. The tinsmithing workshops were at the rear in the original Howitt Street Co-op premises, on what is now a car park. As Button & Sons Ltd the ironmongery business opened other shops in the district and continued until about 1950. The tinsmithing business passed to Mr Pettit in about 1934 and that business still continues in Bonsall Street. The Maypole Dairy, which was situated here from the time of the picture until at least the 1960s, had what was then a fine new shop front with a large plate glass window.

A 1950s picture with the Empire cinema in the centre. This was built in 1920 to the design of architect John Dodd of Long Eaton and had a ballroom as well as an auditorium. In 1924 the owners became insolvent and it closed for six months. The new owners re-equipped it with second-hand seating, so although it was the town's newest cinema it was the least comfortable. The building was demolished in 1961 to make way for Tesco, the town's first supermarket. This ghastly replacement has been slightly improved since becoming W.H. Smith in succession to Preedys. The large three-storey building was Henshall's (wine and spirit merchant) which was replaced by Boots' uninspired structure in about 1964. Woolworths is still there but Currys has been replaced by New Look and Rose's shoe shop closed in 2003.

On the left is seen the Long Eaton post office of 1894, a building which was demolished after the replacement was opened in Tamworth Road in 1959. The Pearl Assurance is one of the better buildings of that period, even though it fails either to be in keeping with its neighbours or to be of special interest. Happily, Express Dry Cleaning has thoughtfully re-used most of the original fascia and shop front. Could George Mason's delightful shop front perhaps be hidden behind the present monstrous abomination?

The main interest in this picture is the row of almshouses, pictured just before they were demolished (shuttered windows) to make way for Central Chambers of 1909. The six almshouses were built in 1858 for a cost of £88 subscribed by townsmen. These replacements for earlier parish poor houses were built on the High Street before it became apparent that the town would expand so rapidly during the following forty years. Were the displaced paupers sent to the workhouse at Shardlow? No provision was made by the town for this type of accommodation until the bungalows were built near the swimming pool in Station Road during the 1930s. The odd piece of street furniture in the foreground is probably a pipe for filling water carts.

Zion Methodist chapel of 1874 with the schoolroom of 1882 on the right. The church was demolished in 1961 when the congregations of this chapel and Mount Tabor in the Market Place decided to merge with the Central Methodist (later Trinity) chapel in Cross Street. In recent years Trinity chapel was allowed to deteriorate and very regrettably, in 2003, the Erewash Borough Council permitted demolition of this very fine classical building. There is no need to comment on the architectural quality of the shops which replaced the Zion chapel.

The building with the spire is the High Street School, the first school to be erected by the Long Eaton School Board. It was opened in 1876 to cater for 600 children but owing to the rapidly rising population it was soon too small and others followed quickly: Derby Road in 1885 and Sawley (Tamworth) Road in 1893. In the centre is the 'old' Central Co-op premises of 1877 with its interesting cast-iron arcading. The building was replaced by the fine modernist Emporium building in 1934. After the school was replaced by Grange School in 1938 the Co-op bought the building and used it until it extended the Emporium over the site in about 1960. Most of the shops on the right, which were originally dwellings, have been replaced by tacky 1970s developments.

In the centre is the main entrance elevation of the 'new' Central Co-op of 1900. This building was constructed by F. Perks & Son to the designs of Long Eaton architect Ernest Ridgeway, and shows the Co-operative Society making a grand statement at the height of its prosperity. No longer in the hands of the Co-op, the biggest loss to the community is the large meeting room known as the People's Hall where many gatherings took place during the twentieth century. The steam roller is parked by the Royal Hotel which has suffered numerous changes in name and function during the last forty years. Few people will remember all of them.

On the right are two very decorative buildings either side of Bank Street – named after one of the first banks in the town, which used the further building before moving to the Market Place in 1889. It is highly likely that the architect was John Sheldon of Long Eaton. The lace factory next door was Joseph Orchard's monumental Bank Mill of 1881 (see pp. 48 and 110).

In the centre is Belfield (now Southlands), the house built by Samuel Claye of the wagon works. A large part of the works is seen above and above right of Belfield's grounds. Fletcher's four-storey factory is towards the top centre and behind it is Grainger's New Tythe Street Mills. Centre left is Orchard's five-storey factory and bottom left is Stanley Mills (p. 98). Top left are the first three houses of Chesterfield Avenue, under construction for the gas company in this 1928 photograph.

Main Street, c. 1910. On the left is the wing of Orchard's lace factory with the decorative gable which fronted the street. The continuous attic windows gave good lighting for the mending operations which were usually carried out there. The factory was destroyed by fire in 1971. The houses on the right were part of a development by E.T. Hooley, which was started during the 1890s. On the left the shops appear to have similar windows so may have been built as such, rather than converted. Leopold Dold, a watchmaker, traded here from 1880 until about 1950.

Manor Park, sometimes known as Monkey Park, marks the point where the stream that flows along (now below) High Street and Main Street joins the Golden Brook. The confluence is now below ground because the brook is culverted here too. The railings around the park were removed in 1942, ostensibly to help the war effort. In the background on the right are the old forge buildings of the Manor House Works of S.J. Claye, manufacturer of railway wagons. Two sets of chimneys from the forge hearths can be seen. Light industrial units replaced these 1860s buildings during the early 1980s. The tall chimney in the background belongs to Orchard's lace factory.

3

Around the Centre

Until the town expanded during the nineteenth century most development was
along the main axis of the village. Consequently, much Victorian development was
behind existing properties near the centre. Most of this has now been redeveloped,
not always with much concern for appearances. The Locomotive Inn in Union Street
was demolished in 1973 to widen Waverley Street.

The New Street–Cross Street crossroads in about 1970, shortly before demolition as part of
the extension works to the Jones Stroud factory. The steel frame of the new office block can be
seen towering above the roof tops. Kathleen Jowett kept this corner shop at the time; later she
was known as Nurse Jowett when she became the proprietor of a nursing home. A faded sign
over the doorway reads 'A. Miller, Tripe'. In 1895 Alfred was a butcher in High Street and
from 1900 to 1908 the shopkeeper in Cross Street was Mrs Mary Miller. Below is the view in
the early 1970s. Opposite, top, is the present view.

Right and below: the junction of Union Street with Cross Street. Jones Stroud (p. 44) considerably extended its premises around the former lace factory, firstly with the three-storey building in 1929 and later with the five-storey office block in about 1970. On both sites houses and shops were demolished to make room. This was the start of the elimination of all inhabited houses in the area which now has little manufacturing employment but plenty of roads, car parks and generally characterless modern buildings.

No longer is the skyline of Long Eaton centre dominated by Austin's tenement lace factory in New Street as it was from 1882 until its demolition in 1999. The factory belonged to Jones Stroud, manufacturers of narrow and elasticated fabrics from 1924, and became vacant after production was moved to Preston in 1989. The site stood empty for many years and several admirable schemes were proposed for redevelopment. Unfortunately none of them materialised and the site was cleared (see p. 43). All the town got was a modest retail development in an uninspired shed-type building and a drive-through fast food outlet set in a sterile landscape of car parks.

The Smith brothers, Samuel and Thomas, had been in the lace business before 1846. They prospered and in 1857 built a three-storey, steam-powered lace factory to extend their business. This factory (listed Grade II) still exists behind the High Street as part of a shopping development (see p. 28), and is by far the oldest surviving lace factory in the town. The Smith brothers later extended their factory, the extension being both wider and taller to accommodate the larger lace machines which were being developed. Unfortunately, owing to an 'administrative error' the larger extension was demolished, so destroying important visual evidence of the early development of the lace industry in Long Eaton.

Claye Street may not have changed
dramatically since 1921 but push-chair
styles certainly have. The corner shop owner
during the 1920s was Annie Hassall, whose
niece Molly is standing (above) with her
seated brother Donald. Sally and Leah
Morison are the modern mother and
daughter. The brick spires on Bourne chapel
were removed during the 1960s and the
large building behind, which was a later
addition to the Claye Street National School,
was also destroyed during that decade of
vandalism. Austin's New Street factory is no
longer to be seen on the skyline.

Bourne Primitive Methodist chapel was built in 1873 in Croft Street. The land for the chapel was given by Samuel Claye of the Manor House and within a few years the street name was changed to Claye Street. The twitchel in front of the building was opened up in 1912 to form the present West Gate. When the chapel became redundant during the 1980s, it was converted to the Duchess Theatre. Sadly, the building was gutted by fire late in 2003.

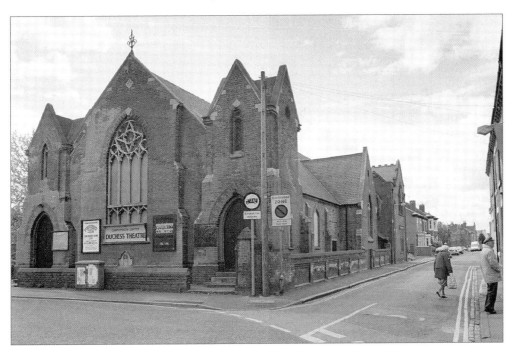

Joseph Orchard's Bank Mill of 1881 and his adjoining house on the right. The whole site was destroyed by fire in 1971 (see p. 110). Below, the area now has the Focus DIY shop and a car park where there were gardens.

On the right the houses are in Northcote Street, pictured above in about 1906 after the ancient charity land on the left, called Poor's Close, was sold for development. The building materials on the site were for the construction of the house and workshop for the plumber Thomas Moss. Later the gabled pair of houses was built for the Nelson brothers who, in 1919, had built a large wholesale vegetable warehouse at the rear. Houses in the centre were in Holme Street and a barrier prevented vehicular traffic from passing. When these houses were demolished during the 1950s the barriers were removed for access to the Romorantin Place flats which were built nearby.

Shakespeare Terrace on Cobden Street, at the intersection of Milton Street and Sandford Avenue, was probably built during the 1880s. The corner shop was for much of its life Mr Hardwick's cobbler's shop. Just to the left of the telephone pole is the name of the terrace but more interesting were the keystones above each door, each with a representation of a Shakespearian character – one was William himself. The Derbyshire Historic Buildings Trust was interested in refurbishing the terrace to modern standards but the local authority insisted on demolition. The replacement block has nothing of interest.

West Park is a 127-acre public park in a central location with lots of sporting and leisure amenities. The earliest part of the park dates from 1905. Pictured here is Children's Corner during the 1930s. Of the equipment shown only swings are now available; the other items then popular are now considered much too dangerous. Slides and hi-tech climbing equipment of the present day are very popular, although gathering a crowd of children together to be photographed using it might be risky. Part of the Sustrans National Cycle Network passes through the park and on the route is a sculpture of Rapunzel, carved on the stump of a tree. One of the National Network signs is also sited here, with directions for Nottingham and Derby.

When the Erewash Valley Railway line was built through the town in 1847 several parcels of land were cut in two. A couple of years later Samuel Claye bought the Manor House estate at the south end of the village and erected his railway wagon manufactory on the west side of the railway line. A thin strip of land had been cut from the estate by the railway and it was here on the east side of the line that Claye built not only a terrace of houses for the workers but also a house for his brother (just behind the wall on the left; see p. 88). Known both as Claye's Row and New Eaton, the houses are viewed here from New Tythe Street. The row with its distinctive chimneys was demolished during the mid-1970s and replaced with better quality local authority houses.

This was Home Farm house in Meadow Lane, until recently situated between the Leisure factory and the derelict Co-op dairy site. In 1917 the farm was bought by the Co-op which in 1929 built a modern dairy on the site. This was demolished in 1971 and converted into the now derelict distribution depot. The farmer in the 1930s picture is Mr Jesson, a Co-op employee. The new building is office accommodation.

The first Baptist chapel in the town is just shown on the right of this late nineteenth-century photograph, the main building being the larger replacement of 1880. The earlier building was erected in 1864, used only as a schoolroom after 1880 and replaced with a much larger schoolroom in 1908. During the Second World War the school hall was used as a recreation and refreshment centre for members of the armed forces, many of whom were based at nearby Chilwell. The chapel was modernised in 1954–5 when the new vestibule was added. The original gate pillars remain but gates and railings went for scrap in 1942.

The Midland Railway's photographer from Derby took this picture in 1911. There are a number of railwaymen behind the closed gates so something special may have been taking place. The shop over the lines was demolished long ago and its site is still empty. The clock on the Co-op tower had yet to be installed and the chimney in the distance on Maltby's lace factory was demolished during the 1970s. The modern hydraulically operated automatic barriers replaced the hand-operated gates in 1977.

Looking south down the Erewash Valley line from the Station Road footbridge, 1911. The central view is of Thomas Fletcher's four-storey lace factory in New Tythe Street, built in about 1875. This factory was the home of Supertone Pianos from 1919 to 1951. During the 1970s the top two storeys were removed and a flat roof added, so it is out of sight in the later picture. In the distance is Claye's Row (p. 52). The shop on the right was Charles Martin's off-licence, tobacconist, sweets and 'choice fruits in season'. On offer were damsons, 1d per lb; Victoria plums, 1½d per lb, apples, 1d, 1½d and 2d per lb; bannas (*sic*), 2 for 1d and potatoes, 2lb for 1d.

4

The Road to Toton

Long Eaton's historic road naming system was very simple – name it after the first place one arrived at. So Nottingham Road was originally called Toton Lane, a name which had become disused by about 1870. The stadium was rebuilt as a greyhound track in 1928 and after the Second World War was used for speedway and stock car racing. The whole area is now derelict and the adjoining Pavilion public house was recently destroyed by fire. There are hopes for a new stadium on this site off Nottingham Road (top left).

Erewash Street was part of the estate built by the Midland Railway in 1873 to house its employees, many of whom worked at Toton sidings and locomotive depot. There were eighty-seven houses, forty of which were built alongside the railway line and known as Forty Row. At the end of the row was the Midland Institute (see p. 94), a large three-storey building which was originally a hostel for railwaymen but had a varied existence, having at one time been a private school. Its site is now the Asda staff car park. The whole estate of what were unmistakably railway houses was cleared away in 1973. In the centre of the present view is the Long Eaton police station, which has recently had a pitched roof added.

A 1926 aerial view showing in the centre the Phoenix Mills lace factory of 1909 and the large gas holder which was only taken down in 1987 following a structural failure. At the top left is the part of the Midland Railway's housing estate called Forty Row with the Midland Institute at the far end. To the left of the houses is the railway goods depot. On the right is the LEUDC's Norfolk Road housing estate under construction and at the bottom centre is the farm known as Coffee Pot Hall, situated between the lace factories and the garage, which at the time was owned by the Long Eaton Motor Company (see p. 62). The recent picture shows the Asda supermarket, top left, and the site of the proposed Tesco, bottom left, formerly the gas works.

After the Midland Railway housing estate was demolished the site stood empty for many years until the Gateway supermarket was built during the late 1980s. Admittedly it had a massive bulk, but it was brick-built with a traditional slate roof and was sited near Nottingham Road. After having been taken over by Asda the building was demolished and in its place is Asda's filling station and car wash. The present Asda shed-type building is separated from the town by a huge car park which detracts greatly from the visual amenity of an area so near the town centre.

The Limes, Nottingham Road, during the 1970s, when the house was used as an office by Barton's bus company. The building on the right behind the bridge approach was a corrugated asbestos bus garage sited between The Limes and North House. The Limes was built in the 1870s for Dr W. Mackern, one of the town's surgeons. One of Dr Mackern's young assistants, Dr Dickson, married Mary, the daughter of Thomas Fletcher of North House. They built Mayfield House next door to The Limes in 1888 and lived there for the remainder of their lives. In 1938 the family sold the house to the LEUDC after which it was used as the Town Hall until the new one was built in 1991.

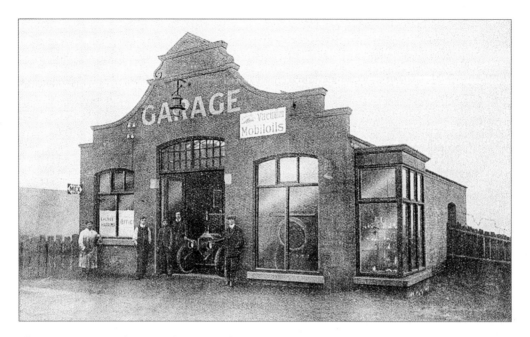

The Garage, Nottingham Road, was on the corner of Conway Street, though the street did not extend to Nottingham Road when the garage was built in 1907 for Launce Harriman. The garage hired rather than sold cars, but it also did repairs, sold petrol and so on. By 1912 ownership of the garage had passed to G.A. Perks, the builder, but in 1929 it was acquired by Mr Wallis, son of a lace machine builder who already had a garage business. Although the business continued as Wallis & Co. Ltd, it was later owned by the Crowe family who in 1936 expanded the works on the other side of the railway bridge and made steel pressings, eventually becoming the Leisure company of sink fame.

Nottingham Road has matured since the top picture was taken early last century and now appears as a leafy suburb. Even modern street furniture here seems preferable to the overhead telephone wires. The view is back towards the town with Grange Road on the left. The large house on the left was the home of W. Pegg, lace manufacturer, where later George Stevenson, the gas works manager, lived for many years. The unseen large house behind the wall opposite was the home of J. Pegg, another lace manufacturer. In the distance can be seen the high-level railway bridge with the signal box perched up high.

A new sewage works for Long Eaton was built at Toton in 1923, so the LEUDC redeveloped the former sewage works on Station Road to become the town's first public swimming baths. Included in the plans were bungalows set on either side of Grange Park for elderly inhabitants. The bungalows were occupied by 1932 and the gate leading to one set of bungalows is in view. The baths were opened in 1935 and although the water was purified it was not heated, so swimming was a summer activity only. A fountain which was situated at the far end of the baths was re-sited to Romorantin Place when the baths were superseded in 1973 by the indoor pool on Wilsthorpe Road. No trace of the earlier baths now remains.

5

The Road to Wilsthorpe

Derby Road was anciently called Wilsthorpe Lane (or Road), but after Trent College was opened in 1868 it was often called College Road, only becoming fixed as Derby Road in about 1900. From The Green to Fletcher Street, Derby Road was largely unbuilt when this picture was taken in 1908. The large Co-op bakery had just been completed and Oxford Street Lace Works was nearing completion on the left. The vacant land was being offered for sale by J. & T. Fletcher's Trustees by application to Clarence R. Ross, Architect, Long Eaton.

The Green, with 'Haddon Hall' in the centre, is in the middle of the upper picture with Derby Road leading off to the left. Below, the redevelopment of the Midland Railway housing estate and the Beeches can be seen, as well as the infilling behind The Hall with the police station, telephone exchange and health centre.

St James Theatre, built in 1907 to the designs of architect Clarence Ross of Long Eaton for local impresario Edward Preston, had stalls, circle, gallery and two boxes. In 1910 it became Vint's Picturedrome, showing films and variety, then in 1916 it reverted to theatricals as the Coliseum. In 1923 it was refitted as the Scala cinema which in 1929 showed the first talkie in town. A fire destroyed the auditorium in 1934 and the subsequent rebuilding included altering the frontage to the present modernist style. Film shows ended in 1964 but bingo was played until 1993. Fire has recently destroyed much of the interior and the site is likely to be redeveloped in the near future.

Looking west along Derby Road from the crest of the canal bridge in 1920 – and not a vehicle in sight. Today even at busy times there are not many pedestrians and even fewer cyclists. Four sets of railings in the Derby Road area were not plundered for scrap in 1942. The school on the left can be seen to have one set. Others are around the cemetery in Lime Terrace, some are near Westhorpe Drive (they were probably buried deep within a hedge) and those around Bethel Methodist chapel (now Oasis Christian Centre) are of a particularly fine Art Nouveau design.

The Lime Grove cemetery chapel was designed by William Knight of Nottingham. His competition entry was selected by the Long Eaton Local Board in 1889, two years after the public cemetery was opened. The chapel, built by Mr Youngman of Long Eaton, was opened in 1891. The building has fared well, having lost only the wooden surround halfway up the spire; it has gained listed Grade II status. The earlier view shows many glass domes on graves, perhaps protecting artificial flowers; unsurprisingly, none survive.

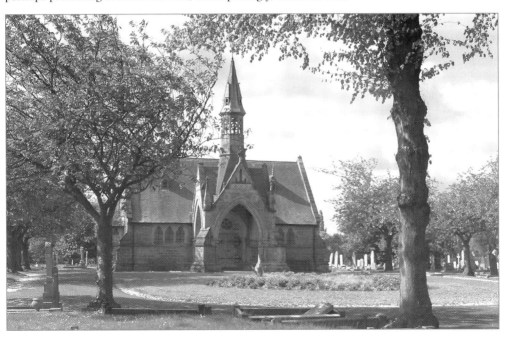

This picture of Derby Road can be dated to 1906 because it shows the Co-op shop on the corner of Lime Grove nearing completion (see opposite). One of the peculiarities of Derby Road is the way that many properties on the left were built with their frontages at right angles to the side streets rather than parallel to the main road. This has led to the added shop fronts being oddly shaped when the dwellings were converted. The building on the left, on the corner of Bennett Street, was for many years a doctor's surgery: Doctors Bloomer, Moir and Rudin among others practised there. Opposite is now the offices and training school of the successful Keith Hall hairdressing establishments.

Long Eaton Co-operative Society opened branch no. 15 on the corner of Lime Grove in 1906. It was built by F. Perks & Son of Long Eaton, using buff terracotta for the detailing. Upstairs, above the grocery and butchery departments, was a reading room. In 1966 the shop was converted to the Society's funeral department. After the Society was taken over by the Nottingham Co-op the building was used by a printer and then in 1992 it became the Chandelier Tandoori Restaurant. Left to right: Sayid Mahmood, Mazhar Iqbal, Prem Singh, Pete George, Tariq Mahmood*, Balhar Singh*, Tahir Mahmood. (*denotes the proprietors.)

Wellington Street School, opened in 1911, was the first elementary school to be built by Derbyshire County Council after it took over from the Long Eaton School Board in 1902. The buildings were designed by the County Architect, G.H. Widdows, who had also been responsible for the County Secondary School on Tamworth Road. Both these schools are now listed Grade II. The exterior of Wellington Street School is little changed but these pictures show how the interior is now very different. The high-level natural lighting has been eliminated in favour of fluorescent lighting and this corridor is certainly bright. The dark glazed bricks have also been painted and the appearance is far less gloomy.

As Long Eaton grew, the parish church of 1868 quickly became too small. St James's mission church was built on the corner of St John's Street in 1886 and St John's was built as a 'tin' mission church on the corner of Granville Avenue and Shakespeare Street. The town was divided into two parishes in 1921 and a new church was planned on the corner of Canal Street and College Street. The proposal is shown here, but although the partly completed church was opened in 1923 it was never finished to the original design by Sir Charles Nicholson. In 1957 a church hall was built on the east end of the site and in 1972 the church was completed, mainly by reordering the interior.

Curzon Street was developed from the 1890s and is still being infilled. This semi was one of F. Perks & Son's standard designs. It was built in about 1900 and is pictured in the mid-1920s. The iron gate and railings are typical of those which were taken for salvage in 1942, leaving Long Eaton (and other towns) with a hotchpotch of replacement walls. Unfortunately, as with many other Victorian and Edwardian houses, the original windows and doors have fallen victim to ill-proportioned plastic.

Red Court, Derby Road, was built in 1910 on the boundary between Long Eaton and Wilsthorpe for lace manufacturer William Johnson, whose machines were in Britannia Mills, Bennett Street. The architect was Osborne Moorhouse Thorp who at that time lived in College Street. The contractor, whose men were photographed, was John Bull of Cobden Street. By 1933 Johnson had left and the house was auctioned. Since that time the grounds and the 'Motor House' have been developed for housing in Rose Court but the building, now without its first floor balcony, is still imposing and is listed Grade II.

On the western boundary of Long Eaton was Wilsthorpe, a farming hamlet which had a population of about fifty or so until it became part of Long Eaton in 1921. Since then most of it has been built over either with houses or the M1 motorway. Only two buildings from before 1921 now remain: Wilsthorpe Lodge Farm and a former cottage in Brookside Close. The older photograph here shows the farmhouse and buildings of Wilsthorpe Farm on the north-west side of Wilsthorpe roundabout during the 1970s. It is unfortunate that some people are now obliged to live within a few yards of the noisy motorway.

6

The Road to Sawley

The road to Sawley, originally Sawley Road, was changed to Tamworth Road after
the First World War when Long Eaton took over New Sawley. Long Eaton County
Secondary School, now Long Eaton School, is in the centre of this 1926 picture and
Sawley Road can be seen winding its way from the Market Place, top centre, to the
bottom right where it is met by the Erewash Canal. A boat can be seen there,
probably discharging coal at Beers' Wharf. Just above that is the LEUDC yard and
fire station. The large building centre left is the Alexandra Rink.

The buildings shown here on the corner of Wheatley's Lane along with the remains of Mr Sheldon's Darley House (left) are shown in 1981. They were all demolished to build what is certainly the ugliest building in the town, sketched perhaps on the back of an envelope if any thought was ever given to its design. Even the construction is cheap; the brickwork on the corner of the lane is overlapped as though it were a back garden wall, rather than a building in a prominent shopping area of the town centre.

This photograph of Tamworth Road during the 1950s shows the row of houses which was demolished to build the new post office, which opened in 1959. Although the sorting office at the rear is still in use, the public service counters have been abandoned in favour of an inconvenient location in the Co-op shop on Cross Street. The other buildings visible in the earlier picture have also been demolished. On the left were the buildings in front of Tucker's Yard (see p. 80). Stables survive at the rear of the present carpet shop. Just in view on the right is the end of Mr Sheldon's Darley House which was converted to three shops, one of which was demolished to build the TSB, now Lloyds TSB bank.

The boys on the left appear to be peering through the gate to South House on Sawley (now Tamworth) Road. The general view is towards the Market Place in about 1910 and the derelict thatched house was on the corner of Beaconsfield Street. Chimney stacks on the New Inn are visible on both photographs, but the rather shoddily built row of shops was a poor replacement for what had once been a rather good house. The sign on the left is that of J.W. Taylor, cab proprietor, whose business was continued by William Tucker after a few years.

Long Eaton Library is undoubtedly one of the finest buildings in the district. It was built in 1906 by the LEUDC following an architectural competition which was restricted to Long Eaton architects. At that time there were enough to provide five entries. The winning entry was that of Messrs Gorman & Ross of York Chambers, and their plans were realised with the aid of a £3,000 grant from the Andrew Carnegie Trust. Apart from the large plate-glass windows, which were at the time very avant-garde, a particularly notable feature is the magnificent stained-glass window at the rear which is just visible through the right-hand window. Although the gates were saved, the railings around both the library and the adjoining school went for scrap in 1942. A tasteful sign would improve the view.

The Wheatsheaf may have changed colour but at least its name is unchanged. It was built in the 1860s, and is here pictured in about 1900, again in the 1950s and, below, in 2003. The site of South House in the centre is now Kwik Save supermarket.

During the early years of the twentieth century there was an obvious need for more than elementary education facilities in Long Eaton. Following a report into education in Derbyshire as a whole it was recommended that a Higher Grade School be provided for the town. G.H. Widdows, the County Architect, designed the building, which was opened in 1910. The wall and railings were built to match those of the adjoining public library and the whole was an imposing sight compared with the drab terraces opposite. The fine original wall has gone but the school still exists behind the trees. Some of the old terraces have gone and in the distance can be seen the flats of Romorantin Place, named after Long Eaton's twin town in France.

In 1911 the original brick arch bridge over the Erewash Canal on Sawley (later Tamworth) Road was replaced because it had become quite unsuitable for even the modest amount of traffic then on the roads. The canal bridge on Derby Road had been first replaced in 1883 and then again at the same time as this one. Both bridges have the same bold cast-iron balustrades and originally had a lamp on each side. The lighting columns on this bridge only have survived. The road leading off to the left on both pictures was originally the only road access to the Sheet Stores (p. 90) and beyond. It is now redundant and many people have extended their gardens by encroachment, making it impassable.

7

Industry & Transport

Railways dominate the town's historic transport system although it was little used to transport the lace on which Long Eaton's rapid development was founded. There are still three level crossings in the town and none of Long Eaton's four old stations is in use. Sawley Junction station has been re-named Long Eaton and a new station in the town is mooted – time will tell. The photograph above shows the cast-iron Butterley Bridge (see p. 92) being replaced in 1902.

During the 1920s and '30s several local bus operators sprang up before being overwhelmed by Barton's buses. J.W. Kirkland operated from this old thatched house in Wilne Road, Sawley, with a service to Broad Street in Long Eaton. Mary, one of Kirkland's daughters, was a conductress. In 1931 Kirkland built a bus garage at the back of the property. Other small-time operators of the period were Annison and Henson. The house in Wilne Road, which appears to have been three dwellings, was occupied during the later 1930s by Bernard Cunniffe and was the place where Plackett's transport originated before moving to Wilsthorpe Road and later to Stapleford. The petrol pump in the front garden remained until long after the house was replaced.

The photograph above was taken shortly before Trent station was closed in 1967. The station can be seen as an island between the lines, bottom left, and the Trent power signal box can be seen under construction to its right. At bottom centre is the Trent rifle range house. From the top left can be seen the railway line which originally ran straight through to Nottingham. After Trent station was built in 1863 the line joined it by a sharp curve known as North Bend. The straight part of this line has now been made into Fields Farm Road and most of the available land is either built over or about to be. The massive warehouse is the Marks & Spencer depot and the only oasis north of the railway is the triangular Forbes Hole, now a nature reserve; land south of the lines is flood plain.

The crossing-gate-keeper's house on Meadow Lane is pictured shortly before being demolished in 1970. It was a typically attractive Midland Railway building but in the 1970s thought to be of no value. The replacement flats on the site have nothing to commend them, but to the right is just seen part of a fairly large house called The Cottage. This was built during the 1860s as the residence of Aked Claye, office manager of his brother Samuel's wagon works. This house is now divided and mostly unseen, but is one of the oldest dwellings in the town.

In the 1960s picture, between the low- and high-level railway lines running from top right to bottom left, the main industrial buildings are those of the Leisure company (both sides of Meadow Lane) and Herrberger Brooks in Meadow Mills on the left. Above the low level-line was the extensive Manor House Wagon Works, long gone. Almost the whole area is now covered by industrial and warehousing buildings.

When the Midland Counties Railway was built in 1839 to connect Nottingham, Derby and Leicester, the railway company built a rail–canal interchange at the point where the Derby–Leicester line crosses the Erewash Canal in Long Eaton. The canal basin can be identified in both pictures. Between the railway line and the basin a store was built for coke which had been brought down the canal from Riddings. At that time coke was used by all locos. The buildings eventually became part of a greatly enlarged establishment which manufactured the tarpaulin sheets which were used to cover perishable goods carried by rail in open wagons. The earlier picture was taken in 1966 when the property was sold by British Rail. Ancient ridges and furrows can be seen in some of the fields.

This was the third site of Long Eaton's railway station. The first was opened in 1839 on Meadow Lane. The second station of 1847 was on the Erewash Valley line on what was then Toton Lane, just east of the site of the Asda petrol pumps. The station was moved to the pictured site on Station Road in 1863. The train in the station is a local service, hauled by a 0–6–0 1F tank engine, built at Derby in 1880 and pictured in about 1910. The recent picture shows an HST 125 in the same position, but not stopping on its way from Manchester to London. Although in Virgin livery, the train is a Midland Mainline set.

When this bridge over the River Trent was completed in 1839 by the Midland Counties Railway it soon become one of the early wonders of the railway. The designer was the railway engineer Charles Vignoles and the structure was manufactured and constructed by the Butterley Company of Derbyshire, which achieved greater fame with the train shed at St Pancras and more recently with the Falkirk Wheel. An account, with detailed drawings of the bridge, was published in the papers of the Royal Engineers in 1840. Each of the four standards above the piers bore the arms of one of the four counties through which the line passed. This fine structure was replaced by an unsightly girder bridge on the original piers in 1902 (see p. 85).

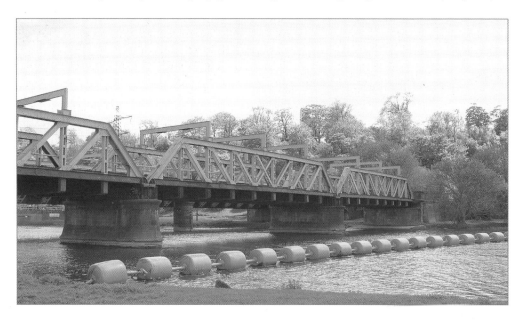

Toton sidings began life shortly after the Erewash Valley railway line was built by the Midland Railway in 1847. The line was used to transport large quantities of coal to the south. Most of the yard is just outside Long Eaton in neighbouring Toton but the impact of the large marshalling yard and associated locomotive sheds was on Long Eaton where most of those employed in the yard lived (see p. 59). The earlier picture was taken looking south in 1948 and shows three engine sheds for steam locomotives. These have been demolished but were situated in the lower right of the later picture (looking north) which shows the newer diesel locomotive depot as well as some of the sidings. The yards have been much reduced because coal traffic is now mostly for power stations and the need for shunting is gone.

The upper picture shows the training centre which was built by the East Midlands Gas Board on the site of the former Long Eaton gas works. The building was interesting, being circular in plan, and was an attractive asset to this town centre site. When no longer required the site was cleared and sold for a future supermarket development. The Midland Institute, below, was built by the Midland Railway and demolished in about 1975 (see pp. 58–9). Both sites are at present barren.

The Long Eaton Gas Company built the large gas holder on land to the north of Nottingham Road after it had run out of space on the gas works site in Waverley Street. Behind the chimney of Phoenix Mills can be seen one of the signal boxes which controlled operations on Toton sidings. All the brick buildings in the centre were constructed during 1940 to manufacture and compress hydrogen gas into cylinders for the inflation of barrage balloons during the Second World War. The balloons were sent aloft on a steel cable to deter low level bombing. After the gas holder was demolished in 1987 the communications mast was erected to carry aerials previously fixed to the structure.

The offices of S.J. Claye Ltd, Manor House Works, Meadow Lane, seen from the railway crossing in 1970. The railway lines in the older view are one of several works lines which crossed the road between the two factory sites. The offices were probably built during the 1860s and demolished during the 1980s, after which a public house named The Tapper's Harker was built on the site. The name is derived from the hammer used by railwaymen to 'sound' the wheels of rolling stock, checking for possible defects.

Opposite Claye's offices were the wheel shops, pattern shops and pattern store. Behind the wall is the Golden Brook which then flowed under the wheel shops and railway line; it emerges again briefly before passing below Meadow Lane. Behind these workshops was the foundry which was built in about 1900 on the site of the old Manor House. Samuel Claye had lived in the Manor House almost until his death in 1887, not having had the chance to live in the new house, Belfield, which he had just built on the west side of Main Street. The recent photograph shows the last building erected by Wagon Industrial Holdings, Claye's successors, before the site was sold. None of the earlier buildings survives.

Shortly after Poor's Close (charity land) was sold, Stanley Mills was built over most of the site in Stanley Street. This lace factory was owned by Samuel Cursley who not only used Messrs Gorman & Ross as architects for the factory and adjoining cottages, but also as designers of a fine house for himself on Derby Road. Stanley Mills is the only twentieth-century lace factory in Long Eaton to have been demolished for redevelopment. It is sad that this has happened because the factory had the most attractive frontage. The datestone (1904) has been incorporated into the development of houses which replaced the factory in 1991–2.

8

Townspeople

The main contrasts between the two sets of group photographs is that in some of
them we don't know all the names and in all of them the fashions are radically
different. But the people themselves don't change; they still have their enthusiasms
for their chosen activity. The picture here is of a street party being held to celebrate
the end of the Second World War. In the background can be seen one of the air raid
shelters in Hawthorne Avenue.

The councillors and some of the officers of Long Eaton Urban District Council were photographed in the Hall grounds on the occasion of the chairman's outing in 1937. Standing, left to right: C.W. Smith, -?-, Percy Fleming (treasurer), Morton Smith, Lewis Patterson, G.N. Windram (valuation), -?-, A.E. Wigginton, W.F. Brentnall (chairman), Harry Raven (surveyor), Miss L. Brentnall, Mr Bennett (press), John Marland, W.E. Crisp, W. Davis, J.H. Feltham (electrical engineer), F. Camp. Front: E.W. Roper, J.R. Davis, C.H. Harding, T.W. Smith, H.L. Burton, Percy Barsby (assistant clerk).

In May 2003 the newly elected members of the Erewash Borough Council who represent Long Eaton and Sawley were photographed in the Mayor's Parlour in Ilkeston Town Hall. Left to right: Ronald Chadbourne, Robert Dockerill, Gerald Hartopp, Garry Hickton, Christopher Corbett, John Marshall, Donna Briggs, Kevin Miller, Bill Camm, Roland Hosker, Howard Griffiths, Margaret Wright, Craig France, Rodney Allen, Brenda White.

The Long Eaton Silver Band was probably formed in 1906 and added 'Prize' to its title after winning many of them. In 1928 the band bought the former YMCA in Salisbury Street, since when it has been the band's HQ.

The bandsmen above display a cup in 1939. Among them are, back row, left to right: Eric Hunt, E. Wiltshire, Jack Edmonds, Ted Eden, Arthur Veasey, Eric Rice, -?-, -?-. Middle row: Howard ?, A. Wiltshire, G. Horne, Stan Bosito, Jack Arden, -?-, Frank Winfield, Jack Earnshaw, -?-. Front row: ? Hatfield, Eric Best, Arthur Marshall, Harry Evett, Tom Henton, Arthur Broadbent, Harold Cox, ? Lawrence.

Below is the 2003 band, now with lots of ladies. Back row, left to right: Lisa Balsom, Kim Larwood, Colin Milns, Steve Berril, Lain Cooper, Mike Larwood, Helen Grimoldby, Robert Stansfield, Samantha Turner. Middle row: Elma Ramplin, James Dennis, George Bayliffe, Sylvia Purnell, Darren Purnell, Roy Varney, Alan Cox, Matthew Dennis, Alex Larwood, Emma Ramplin. Front row: Jason Barradel, Ross Hunter, David Cox, Steve Larwood, Sharon Stansfield (conductor), Melissa Ramplin, Fred Pear, Carl Ramplin, Richard Shaw, Garvin Glennel. Seated: Zoë Cordon, George Ramplin.

Long Eaton Rangers was a well-established and successful team; in 1887 they beat West Bromwich Albion in the Birmingham Challenge Cup Final. Here pictured with Ernest T. Hooley, the financier, is the Midland League team of 1896/7. Standing, left to right: J. Orchard, A. Beard (trainer), A. Clements, T. Meakin, W. Allen, H. Fullwood (captain), J. Fairbrother, G. Winfield, C. Travers, T. Vissey. Seated: H. Hutchins (secretary), W. Dakin, W. Hodgkinson, I. Start, E.T. Hooley (president). Front: S. Bodsworth, V. Grundy, A. Stanion, G. Guy, J. Geary.

Long Eaton United, 29 April 2003. Back row, left to right: Bob Elliott (physio), Glyn Stacy (joint manager), Lee Aldred, Jermain Maxwell, Tom Baker, James Baker, Phil Blasdale, Simon Gordon, Aaron Brady, Dave King (joint manager). Front row: David Thompson, David Lymn, Craig Weston, Marvin Marston, Kieron Heath, Luke Parker, Steve Bowler.

These early cricketers were members of the Queen's Cricket Club, based at the Queen's Hotel in Shakespeare Street, who played on a ground now occupied by the houses of Breedon Street and Curzon Street to the south of Canal Street. Known faces on this 1889 picture are G. Orchard and W. Saxton (standing far right) and Sam Hickling senior, sitting on bench third from right.

Below is a Long Eaton Cricket Club team on their West Park ground in 2003. Standing, left to right: Keith Harrison, Steve Higton, Brett Scothern, Mark Hollingsworth, Neil MacNamee, Andy Hedge. Sitting: Mark Cleaver, Russell Elliot, Steve Hopewell (captain), Mark Brown, Alan Villiers.

After the Second World War the Sawley branch of TocH started a boys' club which met in a room over the shop next to The Bell public house on Tamworth Road. One of the club leaders was Cecil Kingscott and in his garden the boys were photographed in 1948. Back row, left to right: Barry Ford, Stanley Booth, Michael Trotman, Eric Haywood, Keith Reedman, John Salt, Rodger Smith, Billy Geary, Don Hickling, Max Woodward. Fourth row: Ivan Buckberry, Keith Stephenson, Barry Peat. Third row: John Pateman, Philip Read, John Allen, Keith Hawkins, Michael Smedley, Ivan Beers, Peter 'Bill' Birkin, Owen Cripps, Robert Pope, Colin Lowe, Cedric Moorcroft. Second row: Ken Cockbill, Barry Beers, Tony Haywood, Brian Webster, Maurice White, Derek Graver, Michael Dudley, Bill Turner. Front row: Geoffrey Kingscott, Barry McKay, Michael Parker, Trevor Masters, Brian Jeffery, Michael Smith, David Pettifer, Geoffrey Hickling, Maurice Caine, Glyn Brough.

During 2002 a group of survivors reconvened in the same spot to reminisce and be photographed. Back row, left to right: Barry Peat, Eric Haywood, Keith Reedman, John Salt, Rodger Smith, Bill Geary. Middle row: Geoff Kingscott, John Allen, Michael Smedley, Ivan Beers, Bill Birkin, Owen Cripps, Cedric Moorcroft. Front row: Mick Parker, Brian Jeffrey, David Pettifer, Max Woodward, Geoff Hickling, Bill Turner, Robert Pope.

9

Fire, Flood & War

So much effort has been made to prevent the floods that often inundated the town in times past that we now feel reasonably secure. Our safety from fire is in the hands of our fire service which has given admirable service and fought some huge battles in the town. Happily, the effects of war have been relatively slight in Long Eaton, but during the First World War a large shell-filling factory in nearby Chilwell, which employed many local people, experienced several explosions, including one in which 134 workers were killed. The photograph shows Tamworth Road, with the fire station in the distance, taken during the 1932 floods.

After having kept the manual fire pump and equipment in a shed near Heaps shop on Main Street from at least 1855, the Long Eaton Local Board eventually, in 1883, decided to have a purpose-built station. The board had land by the canal on Sawley (later Tamworth) Road and accepted a tender from Mr F. Perks to build a fire station there. It was the first building in the town by Mr Perks who had only just set up in business locally. As well as space for equipment storage, the station also had stables and cottages. After many alterations and additions, these buildings were demolished after the adjoining new station was built in 1978. The new view is taken from opposite the site of the old buildings.

Long Eaton fire brigade's first pumps were hand powered; one of them required a team of thirty-six operators. In 1891, when most of the large multi-storeyed lace factories had been built, the authorities at last decided to buy a steam fire pump at a cost of £600. The newly purchased Shand-Mason steam pump is pictured here in the fire station yard alongside a heap of coal for the boiler, with Lt Sole, left, and George Smith. The appliance was not self-propelled and required a pair of horses to be harnessed. With empty roads, no doubt the equipment could reach most parts of the town as quickly as today's engines. Pictured with a modern Dennis Sabre water/ladder appliance is Leading Firefighter Andy Moore.

Willatt's lace factory in Regent Street was built by Terah Hooley and James Willatt in 1874. It is a large four-storey factory divided into three sections by two fire walls, both of which have proved effective. In 1900 a large fire destroyed much of the centre section which was later rebuilt. On that occasion it is fortunate that water from the town's mains was available because the steam pump was not ready until an hour after the alarm was received. In 1967 the western end caught fire and, although this third was a total loss, the other two sections survived.

Built as the Alexandra Rink in 1910, this building in Broad Street was used for concerts as well as roller-skating until it was converted to the Picture House cinema in 1912. By 1916 the name had changed to The Cinema but the following year it was taken for munitions manufacture as the Long Eaton cartridge case factory. After the war it was used for various industrial and storage purposes until it was destroyed by fire in June 1971. Like Woodland Mills (a former lace factory) in Princess Street, which was destroyed by fire in 1949, the Rink building contained highly inflammable upholstery materials.

Joseph Orchard built his monumental lace factory on the site of the first steam-powered lace factory in the town. Orchard had bought William Bush's factory to expand his business and the new factory was built in 1881 with an adjoining house for himself. The factory was 'L' shaped and built with a tunnel where it crossed Bank Street. After becoming disused as a lace factory, the property was eventually used for tea packaging by Liptons and it was during this period that the building was destroyed by the largest fire seen in the district. The fire started on 28 June 1971 and despite the efforts of over 150 firemen from four brigades, using twenty-two pumps and four turntable ladders, the building was destroyed and it was three weeks before the remains were damped down. The view opposite, taken a month later, shows the inside face of the east wall of the north wing, which had five brick storeys. Behind the wall was Orchard's house. The site is now the Focus building and car park (see pp. 37, 48).

Below and opposite below, the fire raging at between 6.00 and 6.30 p.m. on 28 June 1971. Large pieces of flaming debris can be seen being carried aloft by the huge updraught.

Long Eaton was lucky to survive the Second World War with very few casualties and little damage. Air raids in the immediate area were concentrated on the rail bridge over the Trent which was never hit. The lines were damaged on occasion and the surrounding fields were peppered with craters. The main damage was the destruction of a house at Trent Lock and a pair of houses destroyed during August 1940 in Netherfield Road. Adjoining properties were badly damaged and the fire brigade can be seen recovering personal goods. Sadly, three people died, but it now takes careful observation to detect the rebuilt property.

The worst flooding the town has experienced, measured by the number of houses flooded, was during the period from 1946 to 1948. The floods of 1947 were especially severe: large parts of the town from Sawley to the Market Place were inundated by water often several feet deep. The view here is of Reedman Road where it can be seen that the water was about a metre (3ft) deep and a boat and helpers can be seen delivering essential supplies to people trapped in upstairs rooms. In 1947 food rationing was still in force and relief food and other supplies were afterwards sent from Canada to assist flood victims in the area. The scale of the flooding caused an extensive flood prevention scheme to be quickly put in hand. Flood banks and existing railway embankments have since been successful in preventing a repetition.

This is Shakespeare Street, showing the junction with Bennett Street. As well as the flood water in this 1932 picture, part of the St John's 'tin' chapel can be seen on the left. The floods in the Derby Road area of the town were caused by the overflowing of both the Erewash River and the Erewash Canal. There has been no more flooding in the area since the flood protection works which followed.

The 'tin' chapel was destroyed by fire in 1948. Highly inflammable upholstery materials were being stored there, and they were set alight by arsonists.

10

Sawley & Trent Lock

As Long Eaton expanded it eventually took over two of its neighbours: Sawley in two bites, 1920 and 1935, and Wilsthorpe in 1920. It also took in part of Sandiacre in 1935. Nearly all the land which is available in these places is now built upon and few people would recognise the old boundaries. This is an early twentieth-century view towards Long Eaton from opposite the end of Cross Street, now Wilne Road. Trent Lock, where the Erewash Canal joins the River Trent, has long been a favourite recreational spot, although the relatively new golf club seems to have taken over from rowing on the Trent as an activity. Two public houses, the Trent Navigation on the Sawley side and the Erewash Navigation (now Steamboat), cater for the less energetic.

Tamworth Road near the junction with Wilsthorpe Road, probably during the 1920s. All the buildings shown here were built by F. Perks & Son. The three-storey building had a dwelling, a branch office of Messrs Perks and a branch of the Nottingham and Nottinghamshire Bank. Later it became a branch of the Midland Bank and these uses continued until at least 1939. At some time during the 1940s the top storey was removed and a flat roof added. Later, the building was thoroughly spoilt by the replacement windows and shop front. By a stroke of good fortune three of the other houses have been spared the insensitive window alterations and brickwork painting inflicted on the fourth. How long can it last?

Although this bridge has been renumbered, most people still remember and refer to it as number nine bridge. It is a very well-built stone skew arch bridge which was constructed in 1839 to take the Midland Counties Railway over the Lenton to Sawley Ferry turnpike road. Just out of view behind the tree is another bridge which was put in so that coaches could avoid passing through deep water when the road was flooded after heavy rain. Pumps now keep the water level down. At the side of the signal box is a large stile leading to the footpath to the Sheet Stores. It was along this path that most of the staff at the Sheet Stores made their way to work, many of them having walked from their homes in Sawley.

This postcard is captioned 'Cross Street, Sawley'. It is not known when the cross was removed but it was *in situ*, where the 'Big Lamp' is seen, in 1787; now there is only a traffic bollard to mark the site and even the street name was changed in 1934 to Wilne Road. The three-storey house behind the lamp is the Manor House and all that now remains is its gable wall which abuts the Nag's Head public house. The buildings were demolished during the late 1930s. Further along Cross Street was the National School and what remains of this is now part of a motor showroom. The whole appearance of the street – car parks and a huge crinkly tin workshop – is now more in keeping with an industrial estate than the heart of an ancient village.

The present view is of Tamworth Road, but on the earlier picture it was looking into Town Street from Nottingham Road in the days when Sawley was an independent village. The cottages on the right were typical of many of the domestic dwellings in Sawley during the early years of the last century. Little wonder then that the expansionist LEUDC was happy to take over the more modern 'New' Sawley after the First World War, but was reluctant to have to pay towards the modernisation of the old village. Although Long Eaton's water supply passed along this street from the reservoir in Castle Donington, Sawley still used ground water. The village pump can be seen just to the left of the tall telephone pole.

Plant Lane branched off to the right here, formerly at the junction of Cross Street and Back Street to the left. The Railway Inn may have been so named not because it is anywhere near the railway but because it was necessary to pass by in order to get to Sawley station, a mile away on the road to Breaston. The public house and cottage were demolished before 1914 to widen the road and to build the new Railway Inn. The thatched cottage on the left was not replaced until after the Second World War (see p. 86). The finger post seems to indicate L. Eaton, Breaston, Draycott and Derby to the right. The left sign is indistinct but could only be Wilne, and the sign towards the camera is not seen.

'Back Street, Sawley' is the caption on the old picture from about 1920. Originally this led from the end of Cross Street in the distance to Wilne Lane away to the left and then to Wilne Mills. Now it is all called Wilne Road and since the Nottingham corporation reservoir cut the old Roman road this is now the main route to Draycott. Most of the farms in Sawley were in the village and it was a common sight to see herds of cows being brought in for milking, especially in Back Street. This led to a considerable amount of mess on the road and it was necessary to tread warily. On the right are the Baptist schoolrooms which were used by the local authority until the new school was built in Wilmot Street in 1961. The terrace opposite was demolished before the Second World War.

Town Street, Sawley, was also known as Church Street and is now Tamworth Road. The earliest picture here shows an interesting mix of properties which include the Nag's Head and Red Lion public houses in the distance and thatched cottages in the foreground. In between are three substantial houses and a Victorian terrace. In the second picture of 1988 only the altered centre house and the public houses remain and modern industrial premises have taken their place. Now, the whole of the former Carter's mineral water works has been replaced by new houses – and not before time. The centre of the village with two of its twitchels through to Wilne Road is now hugely improved and gives a visually pleasing vista when rounding the bend into Sawley.

Harrington Bridge across the River Trent replaced the ancient ferry in 1790 (see p. 124). The bridge was designed by Thomas Harrison of Lancaster and built by the Warwickshire contractor John Cheshire. The upper picture shows the three stone arches being dismantled in preparation for the two new girder spans of 1905. In the background can be seen what appears to be a temporary crossing. The bridge is named after Lord Harrington who was the largest subscriber towards the cost of the bridge.

From the tower of Sawley church the earlier picture of about 1900 shows the original stone-built Harrington Bridge and toll houses of 1790. Tolls ceased in 1882 but the buildings were used as a dwelling until the 1930s. Three stone arches were replaced by two steel arches in 1905 (see p. 123). Below are views in 1983 and 2003. In the distance is Marshall's concrete works, started as Sawley Kastone Ltd in 1936 by Les Hogg of Sawley, and the M1 motorway. The house in the foreground is Church Farm House which, before it was altered after 1865, was known as Sawley Old Hall.

Harrington Bridge replaced the ferry which was near the island in the river. All Saints' parish church is visible in the centre with the village north of it. In the foreground is the Sawley Cut, a section of canal which bypasses Sawley weir. In the early 1960s, when the upper picture was taken, a boat yard had just been started which is today a vast inland harbour. In the top left of the earlier picture the M1 motorway can be seen being built.

Trent Lock looking downstream, *c.* 1907. This popular resort, much used by local people, is situated at the junction of the Erewash Canal with the River Trent; it is also opposite the confluence of the River Soar with the Trent and adjacent to the Cranfleet Cut which bypasses the navigation weir on the River Trent at Red Hill. In the background can be seen the bridges over the Trent which carry the main railway lines from Derbyshire into Nottinghamshire and south through the Red Hill tunnels. The Trent Valley Sailing Club was founded in 1886 and its headquarters, opened in 1907, can be seen with much bunting flying – perhaps it was a bank holiday or a Sunday regatta. Just astern of the SY *Ermine* is the old horse ferry boat which transported the canal boat-hauling horses over the River Trent between the Erewash Navigation and the Soar Navigation. Rowing boats are no longer for hire.

The Erewash Navigation Inn is among the oldest buildings in Long Eaton, having been built shortly after the Erewash Canal was opened in 1778. It survived well for nearly two hundred years before suffering the dreadful mutilation which is now evident. Customers now turn up in droves on fine weekends and holidays. In the foreground are four tree trunks which are most likely to be destined for balance beams on lock gates. Many old photographs show these beams as very roughly trimmed, although those of the top gates in the picture appear squared.

Having locked down from the Erewash Canal, the boat will pass under the Trent Navigation towpath bridge into the River Trent. Apart from concrete banks and a trunk-road style of direction sign, little is changed on the waterway since the days of the horse-drawn boat in the earlier picture. The one big difference is the power station at Ratcliffe-on-Soar which is a major landmark. This coal-powered power station, which started generation in 1967, has a capacity of 2000 MW and is thought to have generated more electricity than any other power station in the world. The four-flued chimney stack is 200m (654ft) high.

An empty horse-drawn canal boat seems to be waiting to enter the Erewash Canal at Trent Lock. Perhaps the crew is being refreshed at the Erewash Navigation or dealing with the canal company's officials at the toll office which can be seen on the right. Bunting at the Erewash Navigation suggests that a celebration is taking place – sometimes parties of people were taken on trips by boat, well swept out for the occasion. The house on the left which was the home of Mr Rice, the ferryman, was destroyed by bombing during the Second World War.

Just above the locks at Trent Lock is pictured a pair of well-laden canal boats (in the early twentieth century). Most of the traffic down to the Trent was coal, but the sheets prevent sight of the load. Behind the boats is a canal warehouse with a cottage to the rear, now a canal service station for waste disposal and water. There has obviously been an alteration to the canal here as there is now plenty of room for navigation past the two boats shown in this recent picture. Trent Lock was originally a place where boats were gauged by measuring the freeboard to enable the canal companies to know how many tons a particular boat was carrying.

11

Around the Edges

A number of villages and one town (Sandiacre) surround Long Eaton and a snapshot from most of them is included. Above is a picture of the Blue Ball at Risley before it was rebuilt during the 1930s. Without good reason, the name which had existed for over two hundred years was recently changed to the prosaic Risley Park.

Before 1921 virtually the whole of this view was of Sandiacre. About halfway up the picture, at a slight angle, is the straight line of the former Derby Canal which now divides Long Eaton below from Sandiacre above. The Erewash Canal snakes its way north on the right and Longmoor Lane runs centre left to top right. The earlier picture (below) was taken in 1947 during the building of the Welbeck estate for the LEUDC and the Longmoor School for the Derbyshire County Council. The Crossley Premier engine works is visible in the top right and Springfield House to the left of Longmoor Lane. The A52 bypass (above, top left to top right) was not opened until the early 1960. Although it was built in open land it now passes through densely packed housing estates.

In Longmoor Road, Breaston, pictured in the early twentieth century, can be seen a four-storey steam-powered lace factory which was probably built in about 1870. The factory was owned by the Plackett family and produced warp net, later becoming H. & W. Plackett Ltd, lace manufacturers, until it went out of business in about 1928. Most of the present industrial buildings shown were built by the sheet metal fabricators, W.H. Paul Ltd, during the early 1950s. Modern road widening has considerably altered the aspect of the junction as it is seen today, but the remaining houses on the left are still quite recognisable.

The Derby Canal, which was opened in 1796, passed through Breaston on its route between the Erewash Canal at Sandiacre and the Trent & Mersey Canal at Swarkestone by way of Derby. Unfortunately the canal was allowed to fall into decay and by the early 1940s was impassable. Some stretches contained water but there is not much to be seen in this picture, which shows the Navigation Inn and the Risley Lane bridge. Although the canal was filled in after 1964, much of the route is now a footpath and cycle route. There are plans to reopen the canal and some restoration work has already taken place.

The Chilwell shell-filling factory started filling in March 1916. On 1 July 1918 eight tons of high explosive detonated and wrecked the plant, killing 134 people. The factory was back in production within a few months but the war was over before the end of the year and the factory was mothballed to the state seen in this 1926 picture. The view is to the east with Chetwynd Road on the left and Attenborough Lane at the top. The shed at the bottom is a shell store and beyond is the power station with the chimney. Across the road, the tall building is the ammonium nitrate mill, just behind the TNT mill and mixing house where the explosion occurred. Today the shell store remains but most of the rest is gone and the site of the explosion is now parkland in Chetwynd Barracks. Later sheds date from the Second World War.

The Draycott Motor Company on Station Road, pictured in about 1905, was founded by Marcus Astle of Draycott in 1902 and continued until the Second World War. The car being driven out is not identified but might be a Horbick; the one behind the showroom window is a Lanchester. After 1947 the premises became a yarn doubling factory operated by Astrand Textiles, owned by Marcus Astle of Wilne Mills. The factory was recently demolished to build the present houses in Jardine Court, named after a lace machine manufacturer – Astle Court would have been more appropriate.

This painting shows the Hopwell Hall of 1720, then the home of the Kayes family, which was demolished after a fire in 1957. Nottinghamshire County Council then built a school on the site but that was sold in 1996. The buyer converted the school building into the present country house, which is now an imposing sight on the rising ground above the Trent Valley.

Ratcliffe-on-Soar is just across the River Trent from Long Eaton. Until well within living memory there was a ferry from Trent Lock and a pleasant walk along the bank of the River Soar would take the visitor firstly to Red Hill Lock and then to the village, passing on the way the ford on the River Soar. It was a local excursion which many Long Eaton and Sawley people would make, perhaps doing a little exploring on Red Hill to find veins of gypsum in the hillside behind the lock cottage or to go swimming in the shallows by the ford. The journey today would be more difficult since not only has the ferry ceased operating but also the bridge carrying the towpath from the locks over the river has gone. Flood prevention works on the river have changed the nature of the ford from where in the past it was possible to walk or cycle to Sawley Bridges.

Risley is on the rising ground just to the north of Long Eaton. Nothing now remains of the hall illustrated in the sixteenth-century drawing above but part of a late seventeenth-century building still survives along with nineteenth-century buildings as part of a hotel. Risley Hall is best remembered locally in connection with Ernest Terah Hooley who bought the hall and estate in 1888 and made considerable additions to the property. Hooley, son of a Long Eaton lace manufacturer, attained national fame and fortune as a company promoter and property speculator who eventually overreached himself and was forced into bankruptcy in 1898. He managed, however, to continue living at Risley Hall until the 1930s.

The Erewash Canal passes through Sandiacre where it is crossed by the former Nottingham and Derby Turnpike Road, later the A52 but now, since the bypass, the still busy B5010. The original stone arch bridge is here being crossed by a bus, probably during the early 1930s. On the left is the Red Lion public house and the large chapel of the United Methodist church. During the 1930s the bridge was reconstructed in concrete with iron railings in the Art Deco style and, as they are showing signs of age, refurbishment would be a very worthwhile project for this attractive period bridge. The Red Lion and chapel are now hidden by trees and the latter is derelict.

Just over the River Erewash and in Nottinghamshire is Stapleford. Although this town had an earlier start in the lace industry than Long Eaton it never reached the size of its near neighbour. Nevertheless it did have a significant lace industry and its population supported two cinemas at one time. The Palace, situated on the rise of the railway bridge on Derby Road, opened in 1913, had its façade modernised in the 1930s and closed as a cinema in 1960. It was demolished a short time ago. The Stapleford & Sandiacre railway station buildings were sited on the bridge over the line with access to the platforms by a long flight of steps. The station closed in 1967.

Wilne Mills, a Domesday mill site on the River Derwent, continued the use of water power until the mid-twentieth century. The site belonged anciently to the Episcopal Manor of Sawley and eventually passed to the Earls of Harrington, but it was normally leased. A survey of 1651 describes six mills under one roof, some used for cloth fulling and others for corn grinding. Just before 1789 a cotton mill was erected on the site and others followed. Following a disastrous fire in 1917, while in the occupation of Marcus Astle, the present two-storey cotton-doubling mill was built in 1923–4. At this time water wheels and turbines together produced 300hp. Since 1949 the site has been occupied by a pyrotechnics maker, formerly Haley & Weller Ltd, now PW Defence. Water power is no longer employed.

ACKNOWLEDGEMENTS

Many people have helped with information and photographs used in the compilation of this book and I give them my grateful thanks. They are listed below, along with the page numbers of their photographs (a, above; b, below) if applicable. During the last forty or so years numerous people have either given or lent me photographs and some names have gone unrecorded – my apologies therefore to those people whose photographs are unacknowledged. Unless listed below, all the recent photographs are my own and the others are from my collection. I especially wish to thank my wife Jean and my sister Joan Rippengal for their support and advice.

Aerofilms 13, 38, 66, 93, Brian Amos 87, 89, Donald Allen 18b, Ray Ballard 42a, Morris Borrett 47, 86, 91, 116, Keith Breakwell 103b, Barry Cope, Derbyshire County Library 138, 140, 144, Erewash Borough Council, Erewash Borough Museum 16, 42b, 99, 102, 131, 137, 143, Mike Goy 108, 109, Pat Hassall 46, Alan Heath 32, Peter Henry, Geoff Hickling 113, Councillor Roland Hosker, Ivor Jacobs 138, Geoffrey & Judy Kingscott, Andrew Knighton 14, 20, 35, 75, Long Eaton Heritage Society 48, 59, 77, 136, Long Eaton Library 79, 92, Caroline Marshall 15, Baz Munn, National Railway Museum 55, 56, the late Frank Perks, David Roddis, Sawley Historical Society 115, 120, 123, Sharon Stansfield 101 (both), May Sentance, F.W. Stevenson 139, the late John Sumpter 9, 125, Gordon Wakefield 30, Geoff Whitehead.

The splendid cast-iron railway bridge over the River Trent and the portal of Red Hill tunnel (see p. 92).